C000174363

MARIA GORETTI

TEENAGE MARTYR

by

Glynn MacNiven-Johnston

*All booklets are published thanks to the
generous support of the members of the
Catholic Truth Society*

CATHOLIC TRUTH SOCIETY
PUBLISHERS TO THE HOLY SEE

CONTENTS

All rights reserved. First Published 1997 by The Incorporated Catholic Truth Society 40-46 Harleyford Road London, SE11 5AY Tel: 020 7640 0042 Fax: 020 7640 0046. Copyright © 1997 The Incorporated Catholic Truth Society. This edition is adapted from an earlier CTS booklet by Alexander Gits, SJ

ISBN 978 1 86082 025 0

Saint Maria Goretti

Introduction

Maria Goretti was an eleven year old girl who, in 1902, was murdered in the course of a frenzied, sexually-motivated attack. She was beatified in 1947, in the face of much cynicism from the secular press who did not believe that a child could have shown that kind of depth of faith and only three years later she was canonised and named patron of youth.

Why is she a saint, recommended to us in the 21st century as a powerful Christian witness? A virgin and a martyr! – but what does that mean, how does it help? This all happened nearly a hundred years ago in an obscure Italian village. It involved an uneducated farm girl and a boy, not that much older than her, who was a close neighbour. Some say that this kind of tragedy happens all the time. What makes this one different?

Maria Goretti's story touches on several important themes: the dignity of the human person; the objectifying of sexuality; the importance of Christian family life; how an individual and a family can forgive a person who has done them violence and irreparable harm and how Christian love can change someone's life.

In the late 21st century when many parents and teenagers find it difficult to establish a balanced view of sexuality, Maria Goretti has a contribution to make. In an age when sexual relationships become more and more trivialised we are presented here with someone who, because of her Christian upbringing, regarded her chastity and personal integrity as something worth defending even if the consequences meant harassment and violence.

In an age which demands justice, we are shown that in Christ it is possible to forgive. At a time when no one accepts blame, there is a story of repentance.

This is a story which has often been misunderstood and sentimentalised. Both Maria and her murderer have appeared rather inhuman – she impossibly holy and he demonic. But, as in all these cases, the true facts speak for themselves.

So on 27th April 1947, Pope Pius XII, with all the pomp and ceremony of the time, was carried in a sedan chair into the basilica of St Peter to beatify an eleven year old, Maria Teresa Goretti, who had been murdered during a sexual attack forty-five years earlier. There was a vast crowd there for the occasion: 5,000 adults and over 25,000 children in the basilica itself and many thousands more in the piazza outside. The long ceremony was dignified and solemn. Then, there was a pause, and everyone waited as an old woman was slowly escorted down the aisle to where the Vicar of Christ sat. This was Assunta Goretti, Maria's mother, now aged eighty two. In front of the whole assembly Pope Pius bent down and kissed her hands. This, he said, was the day of the Christian family.

The Goretti Family

Maria Goretti's parents were at once very ordinary and very extraordinary. Ordinary because they were simple agricultural workers with no education nor special talents. Extraordinary because of the deep faith which they both held and which they passed on to their children, as Pope Pius recognised at Maria's beatification.

Assunta, Maria's mother, was orphaned as a child and worked in the fields from a very young age. She married Luigi Goretti when she was nineteen and he was twenty-five. Asked later whether it had been love at first sight, Assunta replied, 'At first and at last.' Although their life together was not without suffering, Luigi and Assunta cared for and supported one another and this example was learned and imitated by their children. In all they had seven children but their first child, Antonio, died when he was only a few months old. The oldest of their surviving children was Angelo, then two years later, Maria was born on 16th October 1890, their first daughter. She was followed by two more brothers, Alessandro and Mariano, and two sisters, Ersilia and Teresa.

Poverty and distance prevented the children from going to school, but their parents brought them up in faith, teaching them to pray and to see God in his creation for they had a great love of nature. The children also shared the responsibility of the work which fed and clothed the whole family. Luigi farmed a small piece of land near Corinaldo a medieval village in the Ancona region. As Assunta put it they tried to bring up all their children to be good Christians. Maria was brought up like the others. She was a docile child but there was nothing extraordinary about her behaviour at that time.

Finally, in 1896, Luigi and Assunta had to admit defeat. The farm could not support them and their growing family. They had to leave. For a while Luigi found work on a larger farm in Colle Granturco, near Rome. It was there the Gorettis met Giovanni Serenelli, a widower with two teenage sons. The owner of the farm suggested the two families go into partnership. This seemed a sensible suggestion as the Goretti family had one worker with several children to support and the Serenellis lacked a real family life. In reality though, it proved to be somewhat more complicated.

After a time there was no more work for them at Colle Granturco but friends, the Cimarelli family, told them they could join them as sharecroppers on one of the farms owned by Count Mazzoleni, near Ferriere di Conca, about eight miles from the coastal town of Nettuno and twenty miles from Rome.

In 1900, when the Goretti family arrived there, the area was uncultivated marshland and malaria was endemic. Count Mazzoleni was a concerned landlord and soon after the Gorettis arrived he brought in what he thought would be most needed – a supply of coffins. As Luigi helped unload them off the wagon he said jokingly 'One of these is mine.' Unfortunately this turned out to be prophetic and sooner than imagined.

Living with the Serenellis

When they arrived at the farm they found that both families were to share the old cheese dairy. This was a two-storey building with the animals housed on the ground floor and the living quarters on the first floor which was reached by a steep outside staircase. The families had a room each to sleep in, but had to share the kitchen/living-room and stairs. There was a lot of inconvenience and trouble, especially for Assunta who had to do the cooking, cleaning and mending for the Serenellis as well as for her own family.

There were other difficulties which also had to be lived with. Giovanni Serenelli was a truculent man and drink made him belligerent. He and his sons read magazines devoted to true sex crimes and would cut out the pictures to put on the walls. Assunta could not read, but she objected to the pictures. Giovanni, however, simply told her not to look at them if she did not like them. It was clear that he was not really interested in trying to adapt to living with another family.

This was a very different family from the Gorettis. The Serenellis too, came from near Ancona but had lived a vagrant life, drifting from one place and one job to another. Giovanni's wife had died in an asylum for the mentally ill, and one of his other sons was still there. The other children had all moved away and Gasparo too, did not stay long at the farm before moving on.

Giovanni's son, Alessandro, was a lonely, moody teenager. His mother had been unable to care for him. His father had left him with a succession of relatives and had only brought him to live with him when he was old enough to work. As a result he was full of resentment about his childhood. Alessandro's first job, when he was twelve years old, had been on the Ancona docks. His conversation was still punctuated by the obscene language that had been normal there. Yet he was attracted to the family life of the Gorettis. He used to sit with them as they said the rosary which Luigi led them in every evening. Sometimes he even joined in. But perhaps because the contrast with his own life was so painful he also spent hours locked in his room reading lurid reports of sexual crimes.

There were often tensions between the two families. The Gorettis tried to live in peace with their neighbours but the Serenellis were the kind of people who resented anything which seemed to interfere with their doing what they wanted in their own home.

Death of Luigi Goretti

Towards the end of March 1901, Luigi began to feel ill. But if he did not work the family did not eat so he persuaded himself it was nothing serious and forced himself to keep going. It was only when he could no longer get out of bed that he allowed Assunta to ask Count Mazzoleni to send for a doctor. The diagnosis was devastating: malaria complicated by pneumonia and meningitis. There was no hope of recovery. The illness lasted ten days. During that time the local priest came to see them several times. He said that often he found the children praying for their father. Luigi was only forty-one when he died. His coffin was carried to the cemetery on an ox-cart. Angelo, the eldest son, sat on the cart holding the coffin to stop it falling off. The other children and Assunta followed on foot. Alessandro Serenelli drove the oxen and, as Angelo later said, seemed to be genuinely grieved by Luigi's death.

On his death bed Luigi had told Assunta to take the children back to Corinaldo. But Assunta had no money and no transport. Besides, they still had a contract as sharecroppers and a partnership with the Serenellis. At thirty-four, Assunta found herself a widow with six children, the eldest twelve years old and the youngest three months.

They had been poor before, but now the struggle was very grim indeed. Assunta later said that neither of the Serenellis ever said a word of sympathy or condolence to them when Luigi died. On the contrary, Giovanni had propositioned her. But, to survive at all, they needed the Serenellis. Assunta had to take on Luigi's work in the fields. To make matters worse, Giovanni and Alessandro were quite willing to let most of the burden of work fall on her. So Maria, at only ten, took over the running of the house and looking after the younger children. Giovanni was very critical of her efforts but Alessandro sometimes defended her saying she was only learning. Giovanni now took control completely. At one point he got a key to the larder and kept it locked except when he wanted something cooked for him. The Goretti children often went hungry, and eventually Assunta had to go to Count Mazzoleni to get a second key to prevent them from starving.

Maria's New Circumstances

The harvest was brought in and sold, but, far from relieving the burden of poverty, Assunta found that the contract left her in debt. Maria was the one to comfort her mother. She encouraged her to trust in God who would look after them. She said that the children were all growing up and that soon things would be better.

Maria was now responsible for all the domestic work. She responded to these new circumstances as best she could given the sufferings they were all going through. As she worked she prayed as she had been taught and this was a great source of strength to her. Assunta was amazed at her. When her hands were free she would say the rosary for the soul of her father. Not that there was much free time. Assunta described a typical day to one of her daughter's biographers. 'She got up with me at dawn before all the others. She prayed at the side of the bed and as she got dressed, but if we were in a hurry because we were late she went on praying while she cooked. Then while I milked the cows, Marietta took care of the chickens and cleaned the hencoops. Then she came back into the house to make the breakfast and wake her brothers and sisters. She helped the little ones to wash and dress. She prayed with them. Then she started the housework, going backwards and forwards collecting this and that that the men had dirtied and untidied.

Then she went to fetch water. If there was laundry to be done, she went to the fountain taking the smaller children with her while I went to the fields with the men.

At lunch-time, she prepared a meal from vegetables she picked from the garden. Then, before the men returned I used to come home to complete the work but towards the end everything was ready.

In the afternoon, she used to iron the linen and clean the rooms. When there was shopping to be done Maria would go and knew how to shop well.

On Sundays we all slept a bit late, but we had to go to Mass and then go again to accompany the little ones. Maria used to keep them near her in church teaching them to cross themselves and genuflect. She also made sure they behaved themselves and looked after their clothes.

Once a week we made bread and that day we had to get up earlier in the morning. Immediately after dinner, Maria would lead her brothers and sisters in the rosary and then she would put the little ones to bed.

But she hadn't finished. She would sit near me and in the light of the oil lamp she would mend the worn clothes while telling me about everything that had happened that day. Then after checking on the little ones she would say her prayers and immediately fall asleep.

I often stayed awake and I would watch her and pray for her. Before turning off the light I would bless her. Could I have imagined a more perfect angel?'

Maria was always very modest in her behaviour and in her dress even in the heat of the summer. Alessandro Serenelli recalled 'She was not frivolous and talkative like other girls. She was satisfied with any clothes her mother made her or any other woman gave her.' Those who knew her said she had a natural dignity and reserve.

Filippo Vari, who was one of Count Mazzoleni's bailiffs, said of her, 'I was always amazed at her gravity in speaking and her grown-up manner.' She was rather shy, and early responsibility had made her very serious. She never had any time to play. Her day was taken up with housework and looking after her younger brothers and sisters. The younger ones always ran to her if they got into trouble with their mother. She tried to take on as much of her mother's burden as possible, trying to make up for the loss of her father. Years later Cardinal Salotti, speaking at Nettuno, said that Maria would have been a saint even if she had not been a martyr because she had the gift of living the holy in her ordinary everyday life.

First Communion

More and more, Maria began to feel the need of the Eucharist. She begged to be able to make her First Communion. There were many obstacles to this. Maria was only ten years old and at that time children made their First Communion at twelve. Besides she could not read and had had no instruction other than that given to her by her parents and in the homilies at Mass. There was no free time, no money for a dress or veil but Maria was sure that God would provide for her. She knew a woman, Elvira Schiassi, in nearby Conca who could read and who would help her learn her catechism. A priest also came once a week to prepare the children for First Communion and Maria worked fast in order to have the free time to go to classes. Assunta had to give in and special permission was requested for Maria to make her First Communion early. She probably made her First Communion on the 16th June 1901. When asked later Assunta was not sure of the date although she remembered the event very well. As Maria had expected, God provided for her in every way. Maria's neighbours brought everything she needed, one lent her white shoes, another a candle, someone else a veil and someone gave her a dress, which was dark red with white spots, to wear for the occasion. 'After this', the child said to her mother, 'I'll get better and better.' She offered up all the prayers and graces of her First Communion for the repose of the soul of her father. The Gorettis were too poor to have a Mass said for him otherwise.

She took her life in Christ very seriously with a child-like simplicity. One day, shortly after her First Communion, she had gone to the well, as usual, to fetch water for the household. While she was filling her jug, she overheard the bandying of obscene jokes between a young man and one of the girls who had recently made her First Communion with her. Maria was shocked that the girl had forgotten her Communion so easily, and upset by the lack of respect they had shown one another. She complained to her mother who sensibly told her to let it go in one ear and out the other, never to get involved in such exchanges herself, and to entrust herself in all dangers to Our Lady.

Troubles with Alessandro

While everyday life went on as usual, Maria was having to face a frightening domestic situation. Assunta continued to work in the fields with the two Serenellis and Maria worked in the home from morning till night, cleaning, cooking, and repairing clothes. Assunta said 'Sometimes I shouted at her because my worries made me irritable. Marietta accepted the shouting calmly and continued the housework without sulking.'

But Alessandro Serenelli was beginning to see her differently. He started to pester her and insinuate himself into her consciousness. First he tried flattery, but he quickly realised this would not work. Then one afternoon in June 1902, when work was in progress in the fields, Maria was surprised to see Alessandro returning to the house. He said that he wanted her to have sex with him. She refused. A few days later the same thing happened again, but this time he grabbed her. She struggled free and he threatened to kill her if she breathed a word about what had happened to anyone. Maria was so afraid that she locked herself in the bedroom and did not dare go into the kitchen, even to prepare the soup for lunch, in case he came back. When Assunta came home tired and hungry she scolded Maria sharply for not having cooked and Alessandro sat and made fun of her.

Maria did not tell anyone about what had happened but we know from Alessandro Serenelli's testimony that she began praying even more than before and found consolation and courage from it. Alessandro also noticed that Maria tried not to be alone with him. She avoided him as much as was possible for two people who lived in the same house. Assunta noticed that Alessandro was treating Maria very harshly and giving her all the heavy work to do. Maria sometimes remonstrated with him and on occasion she was reduced to tears. Her mother comforted her by saying that shortly Alessandro would be called up to do his military service. Maria started to ask Assunta not to leave her alone in the house but Assunta could never get a satisfactory answer as to why so she thought it was just adolescence. She never for a moment suspected that her eleven year old daughter was in sexual danger.

The Day of the Attack

On the morning of 5th July 1902, a Saturday, Maria made arrangements with Teresa Cimarelli to go to communion the next day. She seemed calmer. Over lunch arrangements were made to thresh the beans that afternoon which would involve everyone except Maria and her youngest sister Teresa who was under two years old. Alessandro then told Maria that he had left a shirt for her to repair. It was on his bed. Maria did not reply, so her mother called her attention and repeated what he had said. Maria was obliged to say she would go and get it and mend it that afternoon.

After lunch Giovanni who was weak from malaria went to sleep at the bottom of the stairs. The others went to the threshing floor which was about a hundred yards from the house. Maria got Alessandro's shirt and her sleeping sister and went to sit at the top of the stairs where she could be seen. Alessandro and Angelo were on the threshing machine and Assunta and the children were sorting the beans. Nearby the Cimarellis were doing the same. It was a hot day and the workers were sweating. Alessandro told Assunta that he had forgotten his handkerchief and had to go back to get it. He jumped down from the thresher and asked Assunta to take his place. He went to the house and ran up the stairs past his sleeping father and past Maria and into the storeroom. There he got a sharp metal implement about ten inches long. This was a punch, a needle-like blade with a wooden handle, which Luigi had bought to sew brooms. Coming out into the kitchen he called to Maria to come in. 'What for?' 'Just come in'. When she would not, he went out and pulled her off the stairs although she grabbed hold of the banister and called for help. But despite the fact that the workers were not far away, none could hear her over the noise of the threshing.

Alessandro had counted on this. Pulling her into the kitchen, he kicked the door shut. He demanded that she have sex with him. She said, 'No God doesn't want this. If you do this you'll go to hell.' He threatened her with the blade but she continued to refuse. Maria was under twelve years old and Alessandro was twenty; if he had wanted to force her he had the physical strength to have done so. But somehow he wanted her agreement no matter under how much duress or threat it was obtained. She would not. In a frenzy he began to drive the punch into her again and again stabbing and slashing 'as though she were a piece of wood', as he later described it. Maria fell to the floor and tried to pull her ripped clothes over her body. She called for her mother, then she said, 'I'm dying. God help me.' Incredibly, she started crawling towards the door, calling to Alessandro's father, 'Giovanni, come up. Alessandro has killed me.' Alessandro panicked, and grabbing her round the throat, stabbed her in the back in the region of her heart. He let her fall to the floor. At last she was silent. He threw the punch behind a piece of furniture and went into his own room. Locking the door and lying down on the bed, he pretended to be asleep.

Maria Mortally Wounded

By this time, the baby, Teresa, had woken up and was crying loudly. At last her crying reached her mother who, surprised that Maria had not come to get the baby, began to feel uneasy. She had not taken much notice when Alessandro did not come back, as she was used to the Serenellis leaving her with all the work to do. Assunta sent Mariano to see what was happening and to make sure the baby did not fall down the stairs.

Just then she saw Giovanni rush upstairs, but instead of picking up Teresa he went into the kitchen. He later said he had been woken by the baby's screams but then had heard Maria calling him. He ran out onto the stairs again and gave the alarm. Assunta and all those working nearby came running. Their neighbour, Mario Cimarelli, was the first to reach the house closely followed by his wife Teresa, and Assunta. Giovanni said to Mario, 'She says Alessandro has murdered her but he isn't here.' Then to Assunta he said, 'It's your Alessandro she means not mine.' Alessandro Goretti, Maria's brother, who was seven years old, was with the other children. Assunta and Teresa Cimarelli lifted Maria onto a bed. At first they could not see what had happened but when they helped her off with her dress they saw she was covered in blood from the slowly bleeding stab wounds, which were very small but very deep. Her underwear had to be cut off, as it was sticking to her body. When they asked her what had happened she told them, 'It was Alessandro. He wanted me to do something bad but I said no, Alessandro, you'll go to hell. He hit me. He wounded me all over.'

Later, at the request of the police, Assunta asked Maria if Alessandro had ever troubled her before. 'Yes, twice.' 'Why didn't you tell me?' 'I was ashamed. I didn't know how to tell you. He said he would kill me if I told but he's killed me anyway.'

Mario Cimarelli ran to get the police and an ambulance and his brother, Domenico, went to tell Count Mazzoleni what had happened and to borrow a horse to go and fetch a doctor. Word of the tragedy spread like wildfire and, in a short while, an angry mob had begun to gather at the door of the farmhouse. Someone found the weapon. It had a white handle and the blood-stains showed up starkly. It was only then that they realised Alessandro was in the house. The workers began beating on his door, but it was heavy and bolted. It would not open until one woman, Rita Comparini, became so incensed that she burst it open with a violent kick. The crowd would have taken matters into their own hands if Count Mazzoleni had not arrived at that moment with armed guards. Feelings were running so high that they were afraid to take Alessandro out of the room. They feared not only for his life but for their own. They stayed in the room, guarding him from his neighbours and waited for the mounted police to come from Nettuno. Count Mazzoleni's bailiffs, armed with pitchforks, surrounded the house to keep the people out. Finally the police arrived and Alessandro was hurried to Nettuno.

The crowds were hurling stones and shouting 'Death! Death!' all the way to the jail. Giovanni watched his son being taken into custody manacled between two horses. He kept wandering round the house saying, 'It's not my fault. He never had a mother and he never listened to me.' Giovanni hired a lawyer for Alessandro, but then disappeared from the area and none was interested enough to find him again.

The local doctor came, but he could do little. The horse-drawn ambulance did not arrive until an hour later. The neighbours watched as the girl was carried out, accompanied by her distraught mother and Teresa Cimarelli. The country roads were very rough and the ambulance jolted a great deal. Although it was only eight miles to Nettuno, the journey took four hours. At one point Alessandro passed them, running between the two horses.

At eight in the evening the ambulance arrived at the hospital run by the Brothers of St John of God. Maria had become very thirsty, both from dehydration caused by her blood loss and from the heat, but she was not able to have any water as her stomach and intestines had been punctured. At first Maria pleaded for water. When she was refused she said, puzzled, 'Is it possible that you can't give me even a drop of water?' but she accepted it and did not ask again. Assunta later said she herself had only been able to bear it by thinking of how

Christ on the cross was not given even a drop of water but vinegar instead.

Maria's Forgiveness of Alessandro

The doctors decided to operate. The superior of the hospital, Father Martino Guijarro, came to hear her confession. No anaesthetics could be given to her – she was so weak doctors thought it would kill her – so she had to suffer again as they tried to treat her wounds. But when they discovered the extent of her injuries, the doctors realised it was hopeless. All her internal organs had been damaged even her heart. The operation lasted two hours. She had received fourteen major wounds and four contusions, as well as many other less serious wounds and slashes. Still she did not die. After the operation Maria was carried to a bed on the ground floor, but she asked to be put in another bed nearer to a picture of Our Lady hanging on the opposite wall. She was in terrible pain and there was nothing to relieve it. During this time she said over and over, 'Poor Alessandro. He's going to go to hell. Poor Alessandro.' She asked how her brothers and sisters were. She asked to see them, but this was impossible. She worried where her mother was going to sleep. In fact Assunta was not allowed to stay in the hospital and she spent the night in the ambulance. But, what is truly striking from all the accounts is that most of all Maria worried about Alessandro.

At last the parish priest of Nettuno came to see her. This was to be a very important visit. He spoke to her of Christ's death and how he forgave his murderers and asked her if she forgave Alessandro. Maria seemed tremendously relieved and said that she forgave him with all her heart. She wanted him to be with her in heaven. She repeated this over and over with a little emphatic nod of her head. She forgave Alessandro completely for what he had done to her. She held nothing against him. She wanted no revenge. In fact she hoped he would be freed from the consequences of his actions. Later the superior of the hospital, hoping to bring her some comfort, asked Maria if she would like to be made a Child of Mary. This brought her a lot of joy. Father Guijarro hung the medal round her neck. He was to send Maria's name later to the Sodality in Rome and it was they who provided the first impetus to her beatification process. The hospital pharmacist asked Maria to pray for him when she got to heaven and she said she would. Maria now received the Body of Christ for only the fifth time in her life. It was *viaticum* – food for her journey to God. Assunta told her, 'Good-bye, Marietta. Forgive everyone. Pray for us all.'

Towards the end Maria became delirious. She relived the attack of the previous afternoon again and again, and her terror was clear. She begged her mother not to let Alessandro in. Her last words were 'What are you doing Alessandro? Don't! You'll go to hell!' she tried to

struggle out of bed to escape and fell back dead. It was a
quarter to four in the afternoon of 6th July 1902.

Maria was just under twelve years old when her life
was snatched from her in such brutal way. Yet many were
amazed by this young girl. Her courage and her attitude
towards Alessandro were so real and sincere. They saw
Christ present in all of this. Especially impressed was the
parish priest of Nettuno. In his church records he wrote,
'She wholeheartedly pardoned her murderer and died in
the arms of the Lord.' Terrified as she had been, she had
put her sense of right and wrong, the love of God which
she had learned from her parents, before her own life. A
priest who was a patient in the hospital asked for one of
the blood-stained towels used in the operation. He kept it
as a relic all his life.

The Aftermath

Maria's funeral was enormous. People arrived from all
over the area. There were rich and poor, religious and laity,
Children of Mary and members of other confraternities.
Only Assunta and the children did not attend it. A Rome
newspaper which had run a sensational article about
Maria's murder only the day before under the headline,
'Human Beast. Ferocious Murder at Nettuno', reported all
the details of her funeral over the next two days. Maria was
buried in the Nettuno cemetery in a plot donated by the
municipality. Her body lay there until it was exhumed in

1929 and placed in the Church of Our Lady of Graces. It now rests in the church in Nettuno dedicated to her which was completed and consecrated in 1969.

After the murder none of the Gorettis ever entered the house again. That day, Teresa Cimarelli had taken the little ones to stay with her. In the middle of the night, when she went to check on them, she found them lying silently in the dark with their eyes wide open. It was the Cimarellis too who collected all the Gorettis' belongings. Assunta stayed with them until Alessandro's trial was over. Ironically, she was then able to return to Corinaldo. As she was destitute, she was eligible to have her fare paid by the police. Already, Maria had many admirers and they invited Assunta to spend a little time in Rome. Maria's sisters Ersilia and Teresa found themselves with very distinguished patrons. They were sent to school with the Franciscan Missionaries of Mary, arrangements being made by Pope Pius X and the future Pope Benedict XV. A year after leaving school, Teresa returned to join the order under the name of Sister Maria Alessandra. Ersilia married and had children; Angelo and Mariano also. The third brother, Alessandro, died from illness in America in 1917, at the age of twenty.

Alessandro Serenelli

After his arrest, Alessandro still maintained that he was innocent. He was indignant, outraged, that he had been accused. He knew nothing about what had happened. He was being victimised. He stayed some time in the local jail but then was moved to the Regina Coeli prison in Rome, partly for his own safety. After his initial protestations he became silent. When asked why he had done it, he just said he had a headache.

He came to trial in Rome on what would have been Maria's twelfth birthday. He was cynical and arrogant in court. He showed absolutely no remorse, accepted no blame, but when it became clear that the evidence against him was overwhelming, he eventually admitted his guilt. Alessandro's defence was insanity. He said he had killed Maria in order to have a secure job at the expense of the state, so he had had to make sure he was sent to prison. He cited the mental illnesses of his mother and brother, but, after examination by doctors, the court ruled he was responsible for his actions. Assunta was questioned by the judge and she said even then that she forgave Alessandro. Because he was under-age he could not be executed or sentenced to life, so he was condemned to thirty years' imprisonment. He stayed at Noto prison in Sicily from October 1902 to 1918; before then he was briefly in Regina Coeli prison, Rome. From 1918 to 1919 in Augusta, Sicily, and from 1919 to 1924 in Mamona, Sardinia, 1924 to 1928 in Alghero, Sardinia.

For eight years he remained defiant. He even made up a sort of protest song. It was very cheerful and made light of the time he had left to serve – '…only twenty-six more years to serve and then you'll be welcomed home with cheers.' Apart from that, he maintained an attitude of dumb insolence. The only time he ever had any reaction was when a priest came to visit him. He threw himself at the priest shouting, 'This is all your fault. I would have had her if it hadn't been for you and your church.'

Alessandro's Repentance

After many years of living like this something happened to Alessandro. It was something very ordinary and very simple but it changed his life. One night, when he had been in prison for eight years, Alessandro had a dream. He described that in the dream he was in a garden. Then he saw Maria. She was wearing a white dress and was picking lilies. When she had collected a large bunch of them, she offered them to him. He took them and, in his arms, they slowly began to glow like candle flames. It was then, he later said, that he knew absolutely that she had forgiven him. And this forgiveness changed his life. His whole attitude began to change.

From the time Alessandro had been sent to prison his whereabouts had been kept secret but the promoters of Maria's cause had discovered that he was in Noto in Sicily and they wrote to the bishop of the area, Bishop Blandini, to inform him of that. Bishop Blandini then had to overcome a great deal of official opposition before finally he was given permission to visit Alessandro. The bishop spoke to him about the mercy of God, Christ's death for the forgiveness of sin, and how Maria had forgiven Alessandro. After that visit, on 10th November 1910, Alessandro wrote a letter saying, 'I am deeply sorry for what I have done. I have taken the life of an innocent girl whose one aim was to save her chastity, sacrificing herself rather than give in to my sin. I publicly renounce the evil I have done and beg the pardon of God and of her injured family. Only one hope encourages me – that I may one day obtain God's pardon as so many others have.' From then on he was a model prisoner. He was moved to another prison, in Sardinia, and eventually released four years early for good behaviour with the agreement of Assunta whose permission had to be given under law. He had been in prison for twenty-six years.

Alessandro found a job as a builder in Sardinia. He did his work with great care and patience but although cordial towards his colleagues he remained apart. They were curious about him but he would only say that in his youth he had committed a terrible crime and that he wanted to use the rest of his life to atone for it. It took him nine years to earn enough money to return to Italy. The first thing he did was to go to Maria's tomb, then he went to the presbytery at Corinaldo where Assunta was now the housekeeper, and asked her to forgive him. Assunta answered at once that she forgave him, saying she could not deny him since Maria had forgiven him. At Assunta's request the priest invited Alessandro to stay at the presbytery for a few days, as it was Christmas. At the Midnight Mass of Christmas 1937 Assunta led Alessandro to the altar rail to receive communion with her. There was, of course, a commotion when Alessandro knelt to receive communion and so he turned to the congregation saying; 'I have committed a great sin and I ask your forgiveness.'

By this time the cause for Maria's beatification had been taken up and Alessandro was interviewed extensively. The details of Maria's death come from his testimony. He said, 'I knew I was breaking the law of God. I killed her because she refused. She had never encouraged me in any way – not by a word or a smile. The fault was all my own.' Later Alessandro went to work as a gardener in an isolated monastery. He stayed there, shunning publicity and sensation-seekers, until he died, in 1969, aged eighty two. His last words were, 'I'm going to be with Maria.'

Beatification and Canonisation

The Cause for Maria's beatification was introduced in June 1938. Cardinal Pignatelli, considering the wishes of the population of Nettuno, Anzio and Corinaldo in his diocese of Albano, introduced the cause which was promoted by Fr Mauro Liberati. This called for an examination of her life and writings, but most of all, the

circumstances of her death since she was declared a
martyr. There were no writings to examine because Maria
could not write. Over the years many statements had been
collected from those who had known her and the
evidence of the circumstances of her death was given by
Alessandro. She was beatified in 1947 and only three
years later, in 1950, she was canonised.

Two miracles were required for the process of
canonisation. The first was the case of a workman,
Giuseppe Cupe, whose foot had been crushed by a rock
fall. He invoked Maria Goretti and his injury disappeared.
He returned to work the next day. This happened on 8th
May 1947. The second selected miracle took place four
days earlier on 4th May 1947. A woman, Anna
Musumarra, seriously ill from pleurisy invoked Maria's
help. The next day she was completely cured.

Love is Stronger than Death

This is not only Maria's story, it is also the story of
Alessandro Serenelli. Without the perspective of faith it
remains a rather puzzling one. But considered in the light
of Christ, of Christian forgiveness and of love even to
death, it can enlighten and inspire us. The point is not
simply that Maria avoided being raped. She would not
have been to blame. The point is that she chose to be
centred on Christ and chose to forgive. On many occasions
Pope John Paul II has encouraged young people, saying,

'Do not be afraid to be saints.' Do not be afraid to learn who Christ is, to forgive like him. Do not be afraid to see your sexuality and personal integrity in the light of Christ even if that is different from your contemporaries.

When Maria was canonised, on 24th June 1950, half a million people attended and the ceremony had to take place in the open to accommodate them all. Both the president and the prime minister of Italy were present. Also there, was Assunta, the first time in the Church's history that a mother was present at the canonisation of her child. But the most incredible thing is the fact that Alessandro Serenelli was there with Assunta and her family, a witness that love, the love of a Christian for their enemy – forgiveness – is stronger than death.

A world of Catholic reading at your fingertips...

Catholic Faith, Life & Truth for all

www.CTSbooks.org

twitter: @CTSpublishers

facebook.com/CTSpublishers

Catholic Truth Society, Publishers to the Holy See.